Fly Secrets

T0321560

Contents

Written by Clare Helen Welsh

Illustrated by Andrew Pagram

Collins

What are flies?

Flies are insects that fly up, down, side to side and even in reverse!

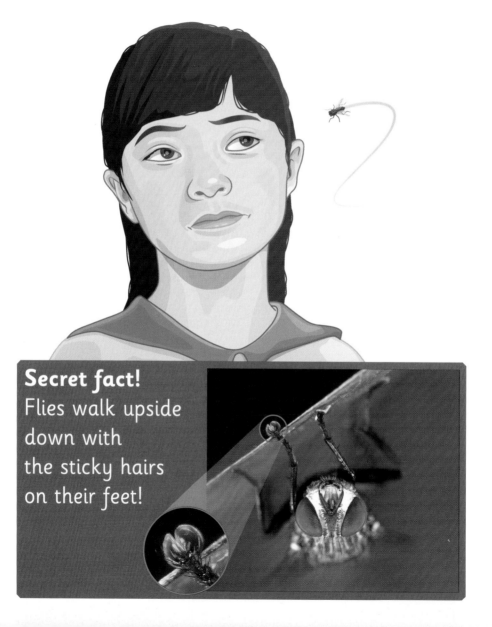

Secret fact!
Flies walk upside down with the sticky hairs on their feet!

Housefly

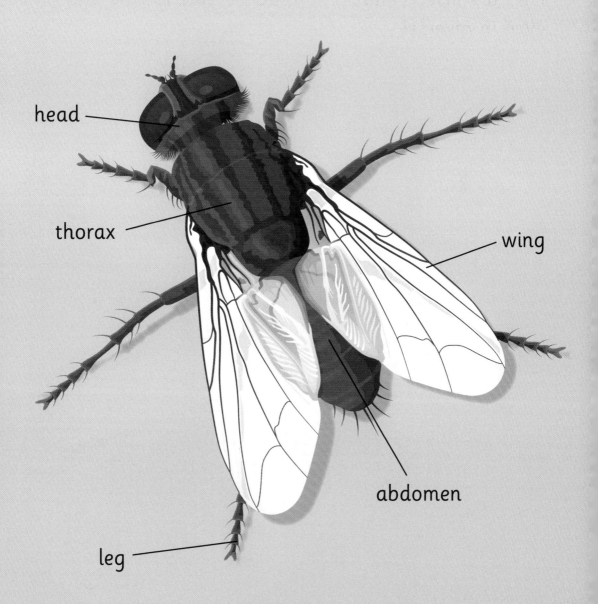

head

thorax

wing

abdomen

leg

Big and small

Some flies are big and others are little. There are over one hundred thousand different kinds of flies.

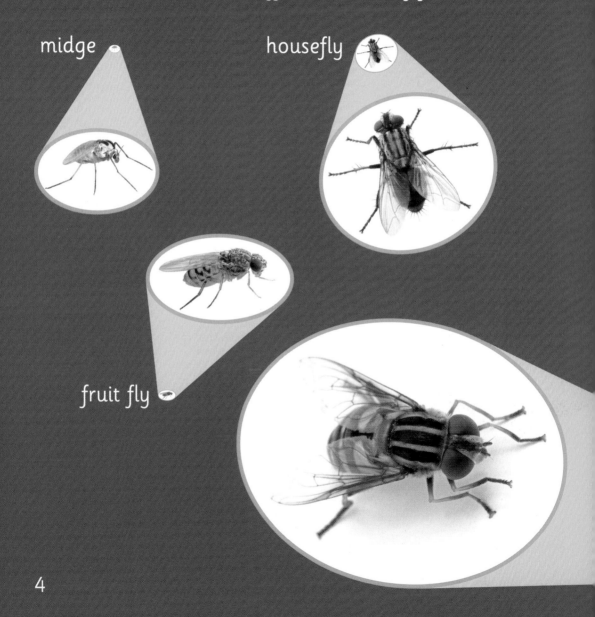

midge

housefly

fruit fly

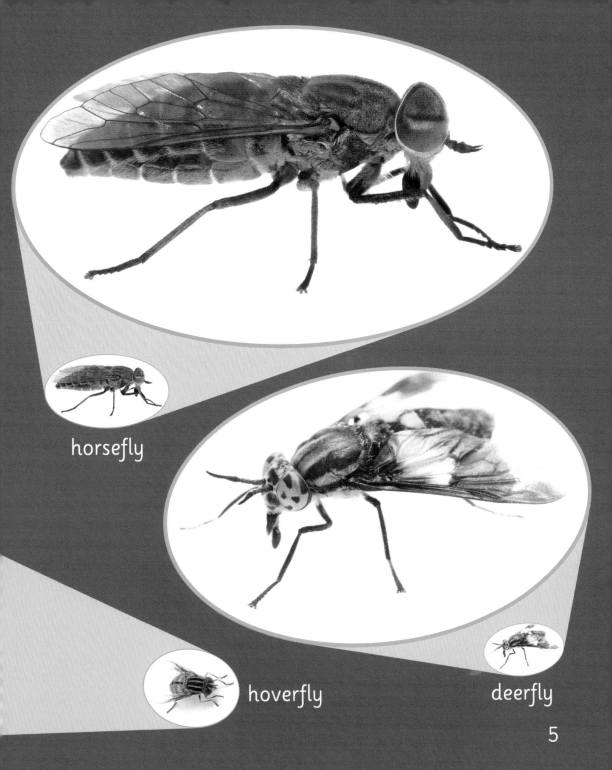

horsefly

hoverfly

deerfly

Catching flies

It's almost impossible to catch flies. They see the world in slow speed.

Secret fact!
Flies can see everywhere,
even behind them.

Dinnertime

Flies taste with their feet. They eat human food, **manure** and rubbish.

Secret fact!
Some flies, like horseflies,
feed on blood.

Flies **vomit** on their food.
This **dissolves** it from
a solid to a liquid.

Flies can suck up their food with their straw-like mouths.

Baby flies

Flies lay their eggs where their babies will have food when they hatch. A baby fly is called a maggot.

Maggots are sometimes born in bins.

13

The life of a fly

adult

pupa

egg

maggot

Secret fact!
Maggots sometimes heal cuts and burns by eating wounded flesh.

Disease

In 1898, in a battle between Spain and America, a higher number of men died from typhoid than from fighting. Typhoid is a disease spread by flies.

Secret fact!
Flies carry germs on their feet and mouth parts.

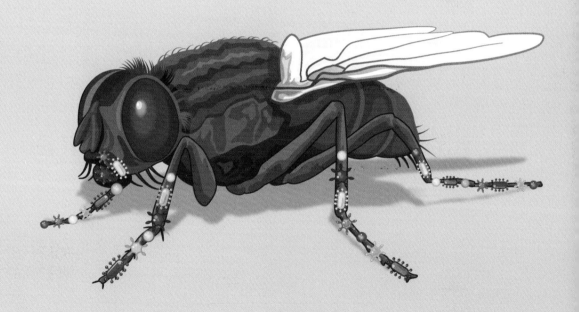

Pollinators

Some flies are pollinators, carrying pollen from one plant to another. Pollen is used to make seeds and new plants grow.

Secret fact!
Midges pollinate the plants
that give us this sweet treat!

Flies as food

Flies are a juicy meal for other animals.

Maybe they aren't so bad!

Spy on a fly

Glossary

dissolves: breaks down solid food into liquid

manure: animal poo

vomit: sick

After reading

Letters and Sounds: Phase 5

Word count: 289

Focus phonemes: /ai/ a /ee/ e, y /igh/ ie, y /ch/ tch /j/ g, dge /l/ le /f/ ph /w/ wh /v/ ve /z/ se /s/ se

Common exception words: of, to, the, into, are, one, their

Curriculum links: Science: Animals, including humans

National Curriculum learning objectives: Reading/word reading: apply phonic knowledge and skills as the route to decode words, read other words of more than one syllable that contain taught GPCs; Reading/comprehension: drawing on what they already know or on background information and vocabulary provided by the teacher

Developing fluency

- Your child may enjoy hearing you read the book.
- Take turns to read the main text, while the other reads the labels and **Secret fact!** boxes.

Phonic practice

- Challenge your child to find as many words as they can on each page with the following sounds:

  /igh/ on page 12 (*flies, fly*)

  /f/ on page 16 (*from, typhoid, fighting, flies*)

  /ee/ on page 18 (*carrying, seeds*)

- Challenge them to think of other words with these sounds written in the same ways. (e.g. *tie, fly*; *photo, fog*; *baby, between*)

Extending vocabulary

- Ask your child to match the correct synonym for each word:

  words: juicy   solid   suck   rubbish   kinds

  synonyms: types   slurp   hard   refuse   wet

- Can your child think of more synonyms for these words? (e.g. *juicy: succulent, solid: firm, suck: drink, rubbish: waste, kinds: varieties*)